PIPSQUEAKS

itsy-bitsy felt creations to stitch & love

30+ Easy-to-Make Animals & Accessories

Sally Dixon

stash BOOKS®

an imprint of C&T Publishing

Text copyright © 2015 by Sally Dixon

Photography and artwork copyright © 2015 by C&T Publishing, Inc.

Publisher: Amy Marson

Creative Director: Gailen Runge

Art Director/Book Designer: Kristy Zacharias

Editor: Karla Menaugh

Technical Editors: Susan Nelsen and Gailen Runge

Page Layout Artist: April Mostek

Production Coordinator: Zinnia Heinzmann

Production Editor: Katie Van Amburg

Illustrator: Aliza Shalit

Photo Assistant: Mary Peyton Peppo

Photography by Diane Pedersen, unless otherwise noted

Published by Stash Books, an imprint of C&T Publishing, Inc., P.O. Box 1456, Lafayette, CA 94549

Library of Congress Cataloging-in-Publication Data

Dixon, Sally.

Pipsqueaks--itsy-bitsy felt creations to stitch & love : 30+ easy-to-make animals & accessories / Sally Dixon.

    pages cm

ISBN 978-1-61745-119-5 (soft cover)

1. Stuffed animals (Toys) 2. Soft toys. 3. Felt. I. Title.

TT174.3.D59 2015

745.592'4--dc23

                           2015008953

Printed in the USA

10 9 8 7 6 5 4 3 2

contents

dedication

For Aunty Elizabeth, who first inspired my love of sewing

acknowledgments

Thank you to my parents, Denis and Roslyn Dixon, for the encouragement, support, and countless cups of tea while I worked on my book. Thank you also for allowing me to create, create, create when I was a child.

Thanks to Aunty Elizabeth, who probably didn't realize quite what she started when she sent me a handmade felt teddy bear all those Christmases ago.

A big thank-you to all the team at C&T Publishing, who believed in my book and helped make my dream a reality. What a fabulous birthday present it was to hear that you wanted to publish my book. A gigantic thank-you to Karla, who helped shape this book into what it is.

Thanks to Yr Ham for casting her eagle-editing eye across these pages and for her lovely encouragement, and thanks to dear Bec Barnes for checking my sewing measurements with joyful enthusiasm.

The generosity of the companies Timeless Treasures, Creative Impressions, Kreinik, Punch with Judy, and Winterwood Steiner Inspired Toys is greatly appreciated.

And last, but not least of all, thank you to my lovely friends, Fiona, Megan, Anushka, Rosalinde, Kendall, and many others, who cheered me on throughout this creative process.

FOREWORD

When I was ten years old, I received a special Christmas present from my Aunty Elizabeth. The package was tiny and squishy. Inside the wrapping paper nestled a felt teddy-bear brooch. He was navy blue, with an embroidered face and a red bowtie.

I never wore the bear as a brooch, but that didn't mean I disliked him. I loved him! Over the following weeks, I examined the bear from top to bottom, side to side, and back to front. I traced around him and created my own pattern. My mother bought some felt squares for me. I cut, sewed, and stuffed until my own teddy bear was complete.

With lopsided limbs and crooked stitches, my teddy didn't look as professional as my aunt's bear, but I felt satisfied. More than that, I felt inspired. Over the next three years, I created an army of tiny felt teddy bears. I made girl teddies, boy teddies, princesses, princes, brides, and grooms. Each teddy bear developed its own unique character.

That's how my love of tiny felt creations began. (By the way, you'll find a tiny teddy project within the pages of this book. He is my tribute—an even smaller one—to the first teddy bear I received all those Christmases ago.)

Nowadays, all sorts of critters run rampant inside my house: rabbits, cats, dogs, elephants, budgies, chickens, koalas, platypuses, and more. And mice … did I mention the mice? If you were to walk into my house today, you'd swear there was a mouse plague.

It fills my heart with pleasure to know my creations bring joy to another person. And I'm passionate about developing children's imagination through play. Within this book you'll find many playful, imaginative, and cute projects. Have a go, and sew one of my designs. Whether the item is for a child or the young at heart, I'm sure it will make them smile.

CONSTRUCTION BASICS

materials

See Resources (page 96) for more information about where to buy supplies.

Felt

Many varieties of felt are available:

- Synthetic felt (acrylic, polyester, rayon, and viscose varieties) is cheap and widely available from craft stores. It is great for children's crafts and for beginners, but if you desire to make high-quality keepsakes, then I recommend a higher quality of felt.

- Eco-friendly felt is made from either recycled plastic bottles or bamboo-synthetic blends. This felt is sometimes stiffer than other varieties, but its environmentally friendly quality is a happy bonus.

- Wool-blend felt is a mixture of wool and synthetic fibers. It is more expensive than the synthetic varieties but still affordable. This felt has a soft, luxurious feel.

- My preference is 100% wool felt—a luxurious and high-quality felt. All of my projects use this variety, from Winterwood Steiner Inspired Toys. It's more expensive, but the quality is worth the extra cost. It's especially useful for children's toys because this resilient felt will withstand constant hugs and touches from little hands.

7

Construction Basics

Cotton Fabric

There are so many gorgeous fabrics around. I choose fabrics with small prints, and I can't get enough of polka dots, hearts, stripes, and sweet florals. The fabrics featured in this book are from Timeless Treasures.

Embroidery Floss

I use stranded embroidery floss (thread) to sew all of my projects together and to add details. I use either one or two strands of floss, depending on the size of the item. Unless the directions state otherwise, use floss to match the felt color.

Needles

Needles come in various lengths and sizes. When you open a packet of needles, look for the thinnest ones with narrow heads. These work best in pint-sized projects, especially when you need to work with seed beads.

Scissors, Embroidery

When it comes to tiny felt creations, the smaller the scissors, the better. Make sure they are good quality, tiny, and very sharp. My scissors have a ¾" (2 cm) blade length.

Scissors, Sewing

Some of the bigger patterns (with straight edges) are easier to cut out with normal-sized, high-quality sewing scissors. Keep a pair handy.

Skewer

The flat end of a wooden skewer is most handy when stuffing little items or when turning something inside out. You also can try Alex Anderson's 4-in-1 Essential Sewing Tool, available from C&T Publishing.

Polyfill

Polyfill (stuffing) is readily available from craft stores and is used in many of my projects.

Beads

Most of my felt critters have eyes made from ⅛" (3 mm) round black beads. Some projects also use seed beads in various colors. These are available at most craft suppliers.

Brooch Backs

Brooch backs come in various sizes. The Doggy Brooches (page 32) have a 1" (2.5 cm) brooch back. You also can purchase very tiny brooch backs, such as ⅜" (1 cm) or ⅝" (1.5 cm), which are useful for the utterly pipsqueak items, such as the Teeny-Weeny Bear (page 81). When in a pinch, you can stitch a small safety pin to a brooch to serve as a brooch back.

PIPSQUEAKS—Itsy-Bitsy Felt Creations to Stitch & Love

Buttons

I love buttons—so many colors, patterns, and shapes! Any button used in this book will be, of course, of the smaller variety, approximately ⅜″ (1 cm). Have fun choosing buttons that you like.

Earring Findings

Earring findings are featured in my Strawberry Earrings (page 85), but some of my other pipsqueak felt items also could be made into decorative earrings. I always use ¾″ (2 cm) French hook wire findings (sometimes also known as fishhook or shepherd hook findings).

Fishing Line / Beading Thread

Fishing line and clear beading thread are stiff enough to make wonderful whiskers for little mice.

Key Rings

Key rings (split rings) are used in my Petite Pocket Pouches (page 22). I use 1″ (2.5 cm) split rings. Why not make some of my other items into a key ring? I suggest turning the elephants (page 42) or Mister Mousy (page 63) into key rings.

Pompoms

Miniature pompoms make cute bunny tails.

Ribbon

I also love ribbons. There are so many pretty designs available. Narrow ribbons are useful for turning my projects into hanging decorations. Wider ribbons are useful for key rings, as well as other decorative features. I used ribbons and twine from Creative Impressions.

Rice

You might think this is a rather strange item to include. But long-grain rice is very useful for weighting down little critters. Mister Mousy (page 63) benefits greatly from some rice inside his innards. Just make sure it is uncooked!

Snaps (Press-Studs)

Snaps (called press-studs in some parts of the world) are useful for the Petite Pocket Pouches (page 22). I use ⅜″ (1 cm) snaps.

Twine

Twine is available in a variety of colors and is useful for turning items into hanging decorations. Try turning my doggy projects into ornaments, rather than brooches. They will look cute.

techniques

Tracing and Cutting Pattern Pieces

Using Individual Pattern Pieces

Photocopy or trace the pattern pieces. Cut out each piece with small embroidery scissors.

- If the pattern piece is large enough, pin it to the felt. Cut around the outer edge of the pattern.

- If the pattern piece is too small to pin to the felt, try holding the pattern piece and felt together between your thumb and index finger. Cut around as far as you can. Put the scissors down. Carefully transfer the pattern and felt together into the pincer grasp of your opposite hand. Return the set back to the original hand, but make sure you now hold it in a different position that will allow you to reach the uncut sections. Finish cutting around the pattern piece.

- Or place the patterns onto the felt and carefully draw around the outside of each with a marking pen. Use small, sharp scissors to cut out, trimming away the marked line on each piece.

Use embroidery scissors to cut out pattern pieces.

Cutting patterns from felt

Using an Iron-On Transfer Pen

Use an iron-on transfer pen to draw the design onto plain paper. Trace with a light hand so the outline doesn't become too thick. (Do not use an iron-on pencil; these don't transfer well to felt.) Place this drawing face down onto the felt. Press lightly and remove the paper.

Cut out each felt piece with small, sharp embroidery scissors. Trim away the markings as you cut.

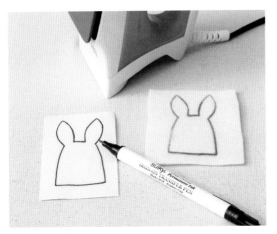

Iron-on transfer pen

Using a Tear-Away Template for Embroidery

I always sew my embroidery features free form, but if you are not confident to do this yet, trace the outline onto white tissue paper. Place over the felt. Stitch through both the tissue paper and felt. When you are finished stitching, carefully tear the tissue paper away. Use tweezers to remove any remaining fragments of tissue paper.

Tissue-paper template

Cutting Circles

I usually cut the tiniest of circles, or other basic shapes, free form. But if you don't like the shape of your free-form circles, you could use a single-hole punch. These come in various shapes and sizes. Circular punches make great eyes or cheeks. A high-quality hole punch will cut all the way through the felt; other punches may cut only part of the way. If this is the case, make an extra snip or two with scissors.

Hole-punched circles

Varying the Number of Floss Strands

Embroidery floss comes in six-strand skeins. As a general rule, I recommend using one strand to appliqué felt pieces or sew together all items under 1⅛″ (3 cm). When I blanket stitch the outer edges of items, I usually use two strands. When I want the blanket stitching to be decorative, as in the mini purse (page 22), I use three strands in a contrasting color.

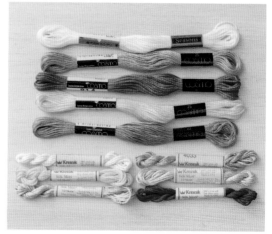

Stranded embroidery floss from Kreinik

Stitching

My projects use a combination of sewing stitches. I find that blanket stitching around the outside edges produces a professional and tidy finish. Sometimes a tail, a paw, or some other felt piece might extend beyond the edge of the body. When this happens, I carefully whipstitch through all layers, including the protruding piece, and then continue blanket stitching. See Glossary of Stitches (page 15).

Stuffing

These projects require small amounts of stuffing. Some need just a pipsqueak amount! The best way to stuff is to do it little bit by little bit. Use the flat end of a wooden skewer or Alex Anderson's 4-in-1 Essential Sewing Tool to position the stuffing.

Stuff items little bit by little bit.

Knotting On and Off

Knotting On

I always double or triple knot the embroidery floss ends. Sometimes I use even more knots, especially when using only one strand of floss. When you start a project, always keep the knot hidden behind the top of the felt.

Keep knots behind the felt.

Knotting Off

It's sometimes challenging to find places to keep finishing knots hidden. Think creatively: Can you find a secret hiding place for a knot? Is there a tail, a brooch back, or a small felt flap where you can hide the finishing knot?

Sometimes there are no hiding places to be found. My little cupcakes are an example of this. To finish off, I carefully make a row of tiny knots around the already blanket-stitched edge. Don't place the needle through the felt this time—just through the blanket-stitched thread. The knots are secure and can barely be seen.

Keep knots hidden.

Tips and Suggestions

Enlarge the Patterns

Aren't scanners and photocopiers wonderful inventions? I realize the pipsqueak world of felt might be fiddly for beginners. My suggestion is to take the patterns and enlarge them to a size you are comfortable with. Once you're confident with a larger size, decrease the pattern size and then have a go at making a smaller version.

Use Glue for Small Parts

I'm a perfectionist (I freely admit it), and I can't help but make everything detailed. It means I like to stitch the tiniest spot of felt, just to make it secure (and as perfect as it can be). But I realize not everyone is like me. If you haven't the patience to be quite so detailed, then grab some craft glue and stick those miniscule scraps of felt in place.

Use glue for small felt parts.

Use Googly Eyes

My felt critters have eyes made with beads or French knots. For fun, you could substitute plastic googly eyes, which are available in various sizes. All you need is a drop of glue, and the little critter will not only be able to see but will also look rather cute.

Use googly eyes.

Use Paint for Some Embellishments

The combination of a dab of paint, a dainty paintbrush, and a steady hand is another way to add features to pipsqueak felt projects. Rather than embroider a face, why not paint it? Or if a felt critter requires a spot here or there, dip the hard end of a paintbrush into paint and make careful splotches.

Use paint for some features.

GLOSSARY OF STITCHES

appliqué stitch
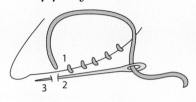

backstitch
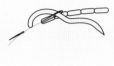

blanket stitch
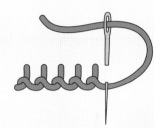

bullion stitch

Step 1

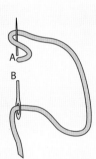
Step 2

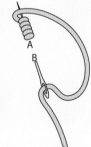
Step 3

Step 4

cross-stitch

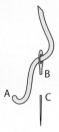
Step 1

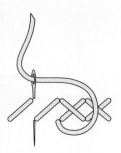
Step 2

fly stitch

Step 1

Step 2

Step 3

french knot

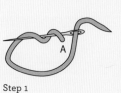

Step 1   Step 2   Step 3

gathering stitch

running stitch

satin stitch

scattered seed stitch

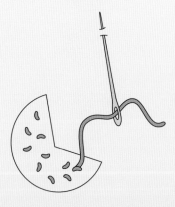

straight stitch

whipstitch

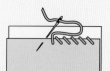

somewhat pipsqueak

2⅜″–3⅜″ (6 cm–8.5 cm)

Pouches, puppets, platypuses, and other petite projects: this chapter features items that are small, but not too small. If you are new to the wee world of felt, then perhaps choose a project from this section first.

Budgerigar Puppet Cozy

This little budgie is a playful hand puppet. He also can keep your breakfast eggs toasty warm.

Finished size: 3⅜″ wide × 3⅛″ high × ¼″ deep (8.5 cm × 8 cm × 0.5 cm)

PIPSQUEAKS—Itsy-Bitsy Felt Creations to Stitch & Love

materials

- **Lilac felt:** 4″ × 7¾″ (10 cm × 19.5 cm)

- **Lemon yellow felt:** 2¼″ × 2¾″ (5.75 cm × 7 cm)

- **Green felt:** 2½″ × 2½″ (6.5 cm × 6.5 cm)

- **Black felt:** 1½″ × 1½″ (3.75 cm × 3.75 cm)

- **Orange felt:** 1″ × 1″ (2.5 cm × 2.5 cm)

- **Cream felt:** 2½″ × 2½″ (6.5 cm × 6.5 cm)

- **Beige felt:** 1″ × ¾″ (2.5 cm × 2 cm)

- **Embroidery floss:** lilac, lemon yellow, green, black, cream, orange, and beige

cutting

Refer to the project patterns (page 21) and Tracing and Cutting Pattern Pieces (page 10).

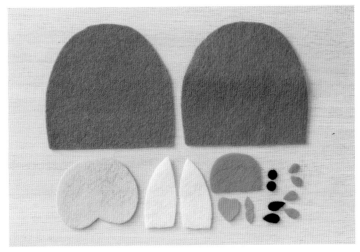

Budgerigar felt pieces

From the lilac felt, cut:

- 2 bodies

From the lemon yellow felt, cut:

- 1 face

From the green felt, cut:

- 1 tummy

- 4 A pieces

From the black felt, cut:

- 2 round eyes (free-form or hole-punch)

- 2 B pieces

From the cream felt, cut:

- 2 wings

From the orange felt, cut:

- 1 beak

From the beige felt, cut:

- 1 beak top

CONSTRUCTION

Refer to Construction Basics (page 6) and Glossary of Stitches (page 15). Use 1 strand of matching floss for appliqué and 2 strands of matching floss for blanket stitches.

1. Appliqué the face, tummy, and wings onto a body. *A*

2. Appliqué the beak, beak top, A, and B pieces onto the face with matching floss. Using 1 strand of black floss, appliqué the eyes in place and embroider 2 eyelashes for each eye. *B*

3. Using 1 strand of black floss, sew 7 straight stitches above the face, 4 fly stitches on each wing, and 1 tiny cross-stitch on the tummy for a belly button. *C*

4. Blanket stitch the body pieces together, leaving the bottom edges open. Knot off.

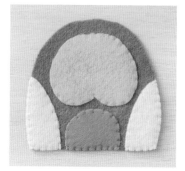

A. Sew face, tummy, and wings on body.

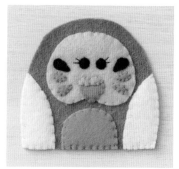

B. Sew facial details.

C. Embroider details with black floss.

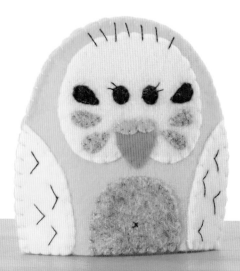

PIPSQUEAKS—Itsy-Bitsy Felt Creations to Stitch & Love

Budgerigar Puppet Cozy
Patterns

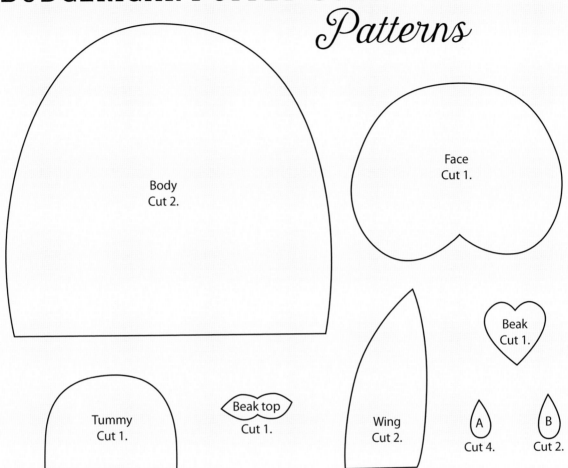

Body
Cut 2.

Face
Cut 1.

Beak
Cut 1.

Tummy
Cut 1.

Beak top
Cut 1.

Wing
Cut 2.

A
Cut 4.

B
Cut 2.

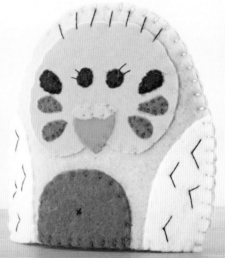

Petite Pocket Pouches

Sometimes a small space is required for carrying necessities. These tiny pouches are perfect for coins, USB sticks, or other pint-sized objects. Why not keep the miniature items featured in this book, such as the cupcakes (page 78), safe inside a pouch?

Finished sizes:

Pouch Key Ring: 1⅝˝ wide × 2¾˝ high × ¼˝ deep (4 cm × 7 cm × 0.5 cm)

Mini Purse: 2¾˝ wide × 2˝ high × ¼˝ deep (7 cm × 5 cm × 0.5 cm)

materials

- **Blue felt:** 4″ × 5″ (10 cm × 12.75 cm)
- **Green felt:** 4″ × 5″ (10 cm × 12.75 cm)
- **Lilac felt:** 4″ × 6½″ (10 cm × 16.5 cm)
- **Lemon yellow felt:** 4¾″ × 6½″ (12 cm × 16.5 cm)
- **Cream felt:** 2″ × 3″ (5 cm × 7.5 cm)
- **Red felt:** ½″ × 1¾″ (1.25 cm × 4.5 cm)
- **Pink felt:** 1½″ × 1½″ (3.75 cm × 3.75 cm)
- **Orange felt:** ½″ × ½″ (1.25 cm × 1.25 cm)
- **2 buttons (any contrasting color):** ⅜″ (1 cm)
- **2 small black round beads:** ⅛″ (0.3 cm)
- **Embroidery floss:** blue, cream, lemon yellow, green, pink, red, black, orange, and lilac
- **Ribbon:** ⅜″ (1 cm) × 2⅜″ (6 cm)
- **2 snaps (press-studs)**
- **Split ring:** 1″ (2.5 cm) diameter

cutting

Refer to the project patterns (page 26) and Tracing and Cutting Pattern Pieces (page 10).

Pouch set felt pieces

From the green felt, cut:

- 1 pouch front
- 1 pouch back
- 1 elephant

From the cream felt, cut:

- 1 pouch top

From the blue felt, cut:

- 1 pouch front (for lining)
- 1 pouch back (for lining)

From the lilac felt, cut:

- 1 purse front
- 1 purse back
- 1 wing

From the lemon yellow felt, cut:

- 1 purse front (for lining)
- 1 purse back (for lining)
- 1 heart

From the red felt, cut:

- 3 hearts

From the pink felt, cut:

- 1 bird body

From the orange felt, cut:

- 1 bird beak

CONSTRUCTION

Refer to Construction Basics (page 6) and Glossary of Stitches (page 15). Use 1 strand of matching floss for appliqué and running stitches and 2 strands of matching floss for blanket stitches.

Pouch Key Ring

Finished key rings

1. Use a running stitch to sew the pouch top to the pouch front. *A*

2. Appliqué the bird body, wing, bird beak, and red heart to the pouch top. Using 1 strand of black floss, attach a black bead for an eye, and make 2 straight stitches for legs. *B*

3. Using 2 strands of floss, sew a button to the top of the pouch front and a snap to the top of the pouch front lining and the pouch back. *C & D*

A. Sew pouch top to pouch front.

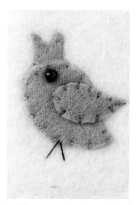

B. Close-up of appliquéd bird

C. Attach button to pouch front.

D. Attach snap to pouch front lining and green pouch back.

4. Stack in this order from bottom to top, aligning bottom edges:

- pouch back, snap side down

- pouch back lining

- pouch front lining, snap side down

- pouch front, appliqué side up

Fold the ribbon in half and place the edges of the loop between the bottom edges of the 2 blue pouch lining pieces.

Blanket stitch around all edges, including the top edges of the pouch back pieces. Knot off. Place a split ring through the ribbon loop. *E*

E. Blanket stitch around pouch edges.

Mini Purse

Finished mini purse

1. Appliqué the elephant, yellow heart, and red hearts to the purse front. Using 1 strand of black floss, attach a black bead for an eye and stitch a tail. *A*

2. Refer to Steps 3 and 4 in Pouch Key Ring instructions (pages 24 and 25) to attach buttons and snaps and to stack the purse and lining pieces together.

3. Using 3 strands of contrasting floss, blanket stitch around all edges. Knot off.

A. Close-up of appliquéd elephant

PETITE POCKET POUCHES
Patterns

Purse front
Cut 1 for outer purse.
Cut 1 for lining.

Pouch top
Cut 1.

Pouch front
Cut 1 for outer pouch.
Cut 1 for lining.

Purse back
Cut 1 for outer purse.
Cut 1 for lining.

Elephant
Cut 1.

Pouch back
Cut 1 for outer pouch.
Cut 1 for lining.

Wing
Cut 1.

Bird beak
Cut 1.

Heart
Cut 4.

Bird body
Cut 1.

Finger-Puppet Friends

*These three little finger-puppet animals love
nothing better than to play with friends!*

Finished sizes:

Rabbit: 1⅝˝ wide × 3⅛˝ high × ⅛˝ deep (4 cm × 8 cm × 0.3 cm)

Mouse: 2˝ wide × 2¾˝ high × ⅛˝ deep (5 cm × 7 cm × 0.3 cm)

Koala: 2⅛˝ wide × 2⅜˝ high × ⅛˝ deep (5.5 cm × 6 cm × 0.3 cm)

materials

- **Brown felt:** 4˝ × 4˝ (10 cm × 10 cm)

- **Cream felt:** 4˝ × 4½˝ (10 cm × 11.5 cm)

- **Gray felt:** 3˝ × 5˝ (7.5 cm × 12.75 cm)

- **Black felt:** ½˝ × ½˝ (1.25 cm × 1.25 cm)

- **Pale pink felt:** 2¾˝ × 2¾˝ (7 cm × 7 cm)

- **Orange felt:** ¾˝ × ¾˝ (2 cm × 2 cm)

- **Leaf green felt:** ¾˝ × ¾˝ (2 cm × 2 cm)

- **Bright pink felt:** 1¼˝ × 1¼˝ (3.25 cm × 3.25 cm)

- **6 small black round beads:** ⅛˝ (0.3 cm)

- **Embroidery floss:** brown, cream, gray, pale pink, bright pink, orange, leaf green, chocolate brown, and black

cutting

Refer to the project patterns (page 31) and Tracing and Cutting Pattern Pieces (page 10). Refer to Using a Tear-Away Template for Embroidery (page 11) for the embroidery details.

Finger-puppet felt pieces

From the brown felt, cut:

- 2 rabbit bodies

- 1 heart face

- 2 paws

From the cream felt, cut:

- 2 mouse bodies

- 2 oval faces

- 2 paws

From the gray felt, cut:

- 2 koala bodies

- 2 paws

From the black felt, cut:

- 1 koala nose (free-form or pattern)

From the pale pink felt, cut:

- 2 rabbit ears
- 2 mouse ears
- 1 mouse tail
- 2 cheeks (hole punch)

From the orange felt, cut:

- 1 carrot

From the leaf green felt, cut:

- 2 gum leaves (free-form or pattern)

From the bright pink felt, cut:

- 2 koala ears

CONSTRUCTION

Refer to Construction Basics (page 6) and Glossary of Stitches (page 15). Use 1 strand of matching floss for appliqué stitches and 2 strands of matching floss for blanket stitches.

Rabbit

1. Appliqué an oval face, rabbit ears, carrot, and paws onto a rabbit body, tucking the carrot under a paw. *A*

2. Using 1 strand of matching embroidery floss, sew 3 straight stitches across the carrot piece. To embroider the carrot tops, use 1 strand of leaf green floss to make 3 long straight stitches. Sew 3 short straight stitches across each long stitch. *B*

3. Using 1 strand of black floss, sew beads in place for eyes and embroider eyelashes, whiskers, and mouth. Satin stitch a triangular nose with 1 strand of bright pink floss. Appliqué the cheeks in place. *C*

4. Blanket stitch the rabbit body pieces together, leaving the bottom edges open. Knot off.

A. Appliqué the rabbit features.

B. Close-up of carrot detail

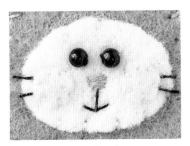

C. Embroider facial details.

Mouse

1. Appliqué the heart face, mouse ears, and paws onto a mouse body. Using 1 strand of black floss, sew beads in place for eyes and embroider whiskers. Using 1 strand of bright pink floss, embroider a French knot nose.

2. Insert the mouse tail, and blanket stitch around the outside edges of the mouse body pieces. Leave the bottom edges open. Knot off.

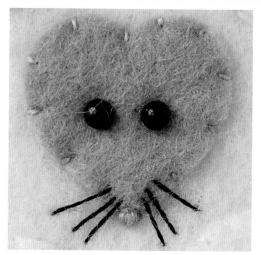

Close-up of mouse face

Koala

1. Appliqué an oval face, ears, and nose onto a koala body. Using 1 strand of black floss, sew beads in place for eyes and embroider 3 scattered seed stitches as freckles on each cheek. (The blanket stitch around the outside ear and body edges will be done in Step 3.)

Close-up of koala face

2. Using 1 strand of chocolate brown floss, sew gum leaves on with a long straight stitch for each leaf and embroider a stem on the leaves. To make the gum blossoms, use 2 strands of bright pink floss to embroider 3 small bullion stitches near the leaves. Using 1 strand of bright pink floss, sew 3 tiny straight stitches against each bullion stitch.

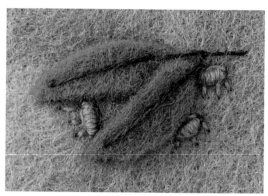

Close-up of gum leaf detail

3. Blanket stitch the koala body pieces together, leaving the bottom edges open. Knot off.

Finger-Puppet Friends *Patterns*

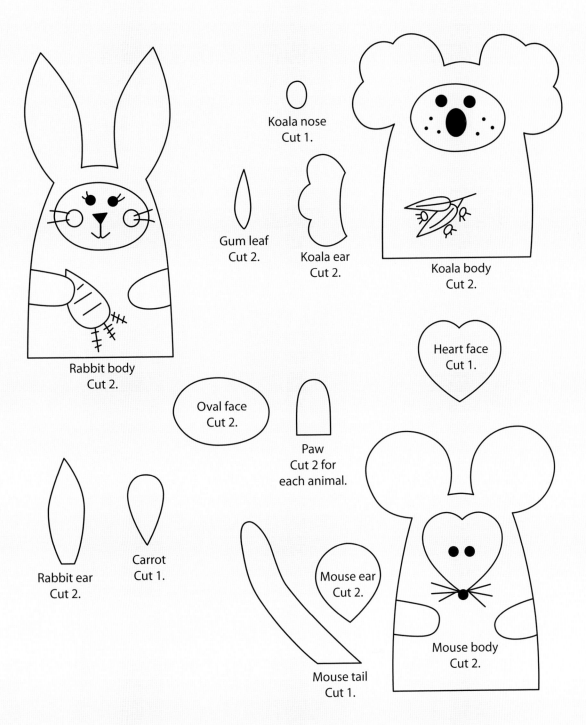

Koala nose
Cut 1.

Gum leaf
Cut 2.

Koala ear
Cut 2.

Koala body
Cut 2.

Rabbit body
Cut 2.

Heart face
Cut 1.

Oval face
Cut 2.

Paw
Cut 2 for
each animal.

Rabbit ear
Cut 2.

Carrot
Cut 1.

Mouse ear
Cut 2.

Mouse body
Cut 2.

Mouse tail
Cut 1.

Doggy Brooches

These happy doggies are ready to adorn your clothes. They like nothing more than to go out for a walk with you and to be admired. With the addition of twine loops, they also make great decorations.

Finished sizes:

Dachshund Brooch:

2⅜˝ wide × 1⅛˝ high × ⅜˝ deep

(6 cm × 3 cm × 1 cm)

Bull Terrier (Bully) Brooch:

2⅜˝ wide × 1⅝˝ high × ⅜˝ deep

(6 cm × 4 cm × 1 cm)

Doggy decorations using twine

materials

- **Rust brown felt:** 3˝ × 7˝ (7.5 cm × 17.75 cm)

- **White felt:** 3˝ × 7˝ (7.5 cm × 17.75 cm)

- **Chocolate brown felt:** 1¼˝ × 1¼˝ (3.25 cm × 3.25 cm)

- **Red felt:** 1˝ × 2˝ (2.5 cm × 5 cm)

- **Black felt:** ¾˝ × ¾˝ (2 cm × 2 cm)

- **Pale pink felt:** ½˝ × ½˝ (1.25 cm × 1.25 cm)

- **2 small black round beads:** ⅛˝ (0.3 cm)

- **10 seed beads:** silver

- **Embroidery floss:** brown, white, chocolate brown, red, black, and pale pink

- **Polyfill**

- **2 brooch pins:** 1˝ (2.5 cm)

- **Twine (optional):** 8˝ (20 cm)

cutting

Refer to the project patterns (page 35) and Tracing and Cutting Pattern Pieces (page 10).

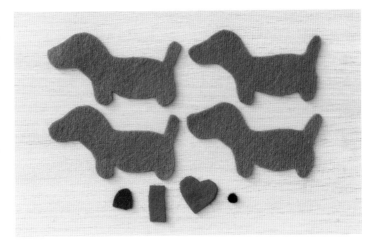

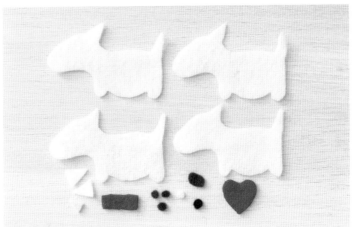

Doggy felt pieces

Cutting continues

From the rust brown felt, cut:

- 4 dachshund bodies

From the white felt, cut:

- 4 bully bodies

- 1 bully eye spot (free-form or hole-punch)

- 2 bully ears

From the chocolate brown felt, cut:

- 1 dachshund ear

- 1 bully eye patch (free-form or pattern)

- 3 bully spots (free-form or hole-punch)

From the red felt, cut:

- 1 dachshund collar

- 1 bully collar

- 2 hearts

From the black felt, cut:

- 2 noses (free-form or hole-punch)

From the pale pink felt, cut:

- 1 bully inner ear (free-form or pattern)

CONSTRUCTION

Refer to Construction Basics (page 6) and Glossary of Stitches (page 15). Use 1 strand of matching floss for appliqué and running stitches and 2 strands of matching floss for blanket stitches.

A. Attach dachshund eye, nose, and ear.

Dachshund

----

1. Using 1 strand of black floss, sew a small black eye bead onto a dachshund body and appliqué the nose in place. With 1 strand of matching floss, whipstitch the top of the dachshund ear in place. *A*

2. Using 2 strands of red floss, sew the brooch pin firmly into place on the back of another dachshund body piece. Use a running stitch to attach a heart over the brooch pin base. *B*

B. Attach brooch pin and heart.

3. Place the 4 dachshund body pieces together, with the front piece on top and the brooch piece on the back. Using 2 strands of matching floss, blanket stitch around all 4 pieces. Before finishing, stuff the tummy with a small amount of polyfill. Finish stitching and knot off.

4. Using 1 strand of red floss, whipstitch the red collar in place and sew silver beads onto the collar. Knot off at the base of the collar. *C*

C. Stitch the collar in place.

Bull Terrier

1. Using 1 strand of black floss sew a small black eye bead, white eye spot, and brown bully eye patch onto a bully body. Appliqué the black nose, brown spots, and pink inner ear onto the body.

2. Using the bully pattern pieces, follow Dachshund construction Steps 2–4 (page 34) to complete the bull terrier brooch, making sure you insert the 2 bully ear pieces layered and blanket stitched together. Whipstitch the ear in place through all the layers.

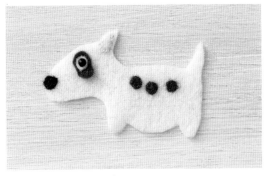

Attach eye, nose, ear, and spots.

DOGGY BROOCHES
Patterns

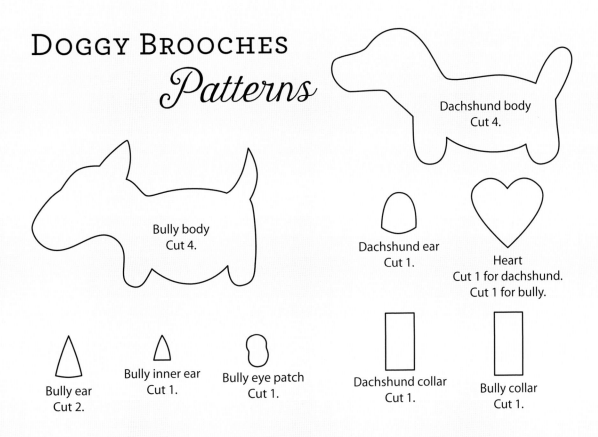

Dachshund body
Cut 4.

Bully body
Cut 4.

Dachshund ear
Cut 1.

Heart
Cut 1 for dachshund.
Cut 1 for bully.

Bully ear
Cut 2.

Bully inner ear
Cut 1.

Bully eye patch
Cut 1.

Dachshund collar
Cut 1.

Bully collar
Cut 1.

Platypus Peekaboo Bed

When he's not swimming, this tiny Australian platypus likes
nothing better than to snooze inside his cozy pocket bed.

Finished sizes:

Pocket Bed: 2˝ wide × 3⅛˝ high × ⅜˝ deep (5 cm × 8 cm × 1 cm)

Platypus: 1⅜˝ wide × 2½˝ high × ⅜˝ deep (3.5 cm × 6.5 cm × 1 cm)

PIPSQUEAKS—*Itsy-Bitsy Felt Creations to Stitch & Love*

materials

- **Blue felt:** 2½″ × 6¾″ (6.5 cm × 17 cm)
- **Lemon yellow felt:** 2½″ × 6¼″ (6.5 cm × 16 cm)
- **Red felt:** 1¼″ × 1¼″ (3.25 cm × 3.25 cm)
- **Chocolate brown felt:** 2¼″ × 3¾″ (5.75 cm × 9.5 cm)
- **Orange felt:** 1¼″ × 1¼″ (3.25 cm × 3.25 cm)
- **White felt:** ¾″ × ¾″ (2 cm × 2 cm)
- **Beige felt:** 2″ × 2¾″ (5 cm × 7 cm)
- **2 small black round beads:** ⅛″ (0.3 cm)
- **Embroidery floss:** blue, orange, red, chocolate brown, beige, and black
- **Polyfill**

cutting

Refer to the project patterns (page 40) and Tracing and Cutting Pattern Pieces (page 10).

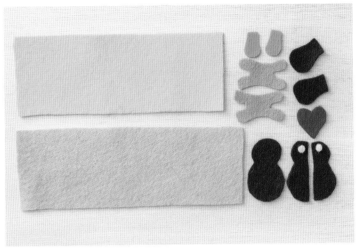

Platypus felt pieces

From the blue felt, cut:

- 1 rectangle 2¼″ × 6¼″ (5.75 cm × 16 cm) for the outer pocket

From the lemon yellow felt, cut:

- 1 rectangle 2¼″ × 6″ (5.75 cm × 15.25 cm) for the inner pocket

From the red felt, cut:

- 1 heart

From the chocolate brown felt, cut:

- 1 base
- 2 sides
- 2 tails

From the orange felt, cut:

- 2 bills

From the beige felt, cut:

- 2 feet

From the white felt, cut:

- 2 eyes (free-form or hole-punch)

CONSTRUCTION

Refer to Construction Basics (page 6) and Glossary of Stitches (page 15). Use 1 strand of matching floss for appliqué and running stitches and 2 strands of matching floss for blanket stitches.

Pocket Bed

Finished pocket bed

1. Appliqué the heart into place on the outer pocket ⅝˝ (1.5 cm) from the end as shown.

Appliqué heart to outer pocket.

2. Place the outer pocket and inner pocket together. Align the heart end of the blue piece even with the end of the yellow piece and fold the even edges up until they cover ¾ of the pocket. Fold the top edges over until they meet the bottom edges. (As it folds, the blue and yellow will meet neatly together.) Pin in place.

Fold pocket edges over.

3. Blanket stitch all the outer edges and inner flaps together. Knot off.

Platypus

Finished platypus

1. Using 1 strand of matching floss, blanket stitch each of the following together: 2 bills, 2 feet, and 2 tails. Knot each off.

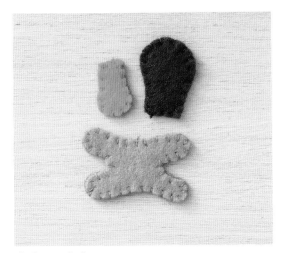

Blanket stitch platypus parts.

2. To make the eyes, use 2 strands of black floss to sew a white felt circle and black bead onto each platypus side.

Stitch the eyes in place.

3. Place the feet on the platypus base. Place the platypus's right side piece on top. Begin blanket stitching near the bottom right foot. Stitch around the platypus side. Whenever you come to a foot, whipstitch through all layers including the foot, then continue blanket stitching.

Platypus construction

4. Insert the platypus bill, place the left platypus side on top, and whipstitch the platypus bill in place. Continue to blanket stitch around the platypus. Insert the platypus tail and whipstitch in place. *A*

5. Blanket stitch halfway up the platypus back. Stuff the platypus with polyfill. Stitch along the other half of the platypus back. Knot off underneath the platypus bill. *B*

A. Stitch platypus bill and tail in place.

B. Stitch and stuff the platypus.

PLATYPUS PEEKABOO BED
Patterns

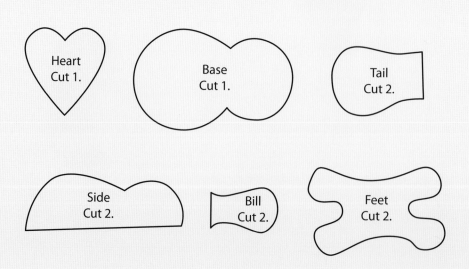

Heart
Cut 1.

Base
Cut 1.

Tail
Cut 2.

Side
Cut 2.

Bill
Cut 2.

Feet
Cut 2.

PIPSQUEAKS—Itsy-Bitsy Felt Creations to Stitch & Love

perfectly pipsqueak

1⅛″–2⅛″ (3 cm–5.5 cm)

There's a lot of critter love in this section, with happy animal families and other playful creatures. Why not expand the families? Enlarge or decrease the patterns so you can add variety to the family members.

Elephant Love

Mother Elephant loves her baby; and Baby Elephant loves his mother. Try making them in different colors, with a variety of fabric accents.

Finished sizes:

Mother Elephant (measuring from front view):

2″ (including ears) wide × 1⅝″ high × 2″ deep, plus ⅝″ tail

(5 cm × 4 cm × 5 cm, plus 1.5 cm tail)

Baby Elephant: 1⅛″ (including ears) wide × ¾″ high × ⅝″ deep, plus ⅜″ tail

(3 cm × 2 cm × 1.5 cm, plus 1 cm tail)

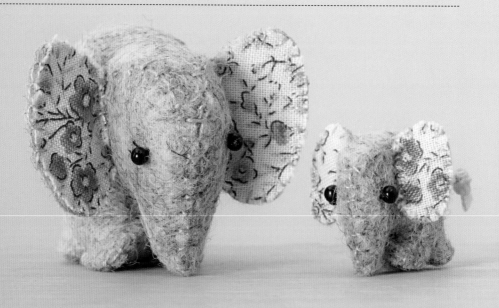

materials

- **Gray felt:** 4¾″ × 6″ (12 cm × 15.25 cm)

- **Bright pink felt:** 1¼″ × 1¼″ (3.25 cm × 3.25 cm)

- **Patterned fabric:** 2½″ × 2½″ (6.5 cm × 6.5 cm)

- **2 ribbons:** ⅛″ × 2″ (0.3 cm × 5 cm)

- **4 small black round beads:** ⅛″ (0.3 cm)

- **Embroidery floss:** gray, black, and bright pink

- **Polyfill**

cutting

Refer to the project patterns (page 46) and Tracing and Cutting Pattern Pieces (page 10).

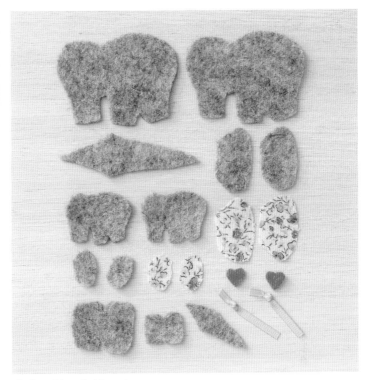

Elephant felt and ribbon pieces

From the gray felt, cut:

- 2 big elephant sides

- 2 baby elephant sides

- 1 big elephant base

- 1 baby elephant base

- 1 big elephant top

- 1 baby elephant top

- 2 big ears

- 2 baby ears

From the bright pink felt, cut:

- 1 big heart

- 1 baby heart

From the patterned fabric, cut:

- 2 big ears

- 2 baby ears

CONSTRUCTION

Refer to Construction Basics (page 6) and Glossary of Stitches (page 15). Use 1 strand of matching floss for appliqué stitches and 2 strands of matching floss for blanket stitches. When blanket stitching the elephants together, don't knot off until instructed.

Mother Elephant

1. Using 1 strand of black floss, sew beads in place for eyes and make 2 straight stitches beside each bead for eyelashes on each big elephant side. Appliqué the big heart to 1 elephant side.

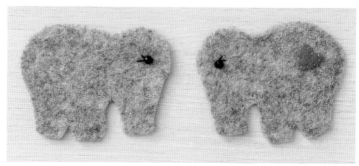

Attach eye beads and heart.

2. Blanket stitch a big elephant side to the big elephant base. Start at the back of the elephant.

Sew base and side together.

3. After the first side is attached to half of the base, continue blanket stitching to attach the other side to the base.

Sew second elephant side to base.

4. Tie a knot on 1 end of a ribbon. Insert into back of elephant. Continue blanket stitching the side pieces together, making sure the ribbon is securely sewn between them. *A*

5. Blanket stitch the elephant top to a side piece. Continue stitching down and around the trunk. Stop stitching after the trunk, but do not knot off. *B*

6. Put some polyfill into the trunk. Bring the needle up and through the trunk, and continue to blanket stitch the opposite side of the elephant top to the other side. When you have stitched halfway along the elephant side piece, stop and stuff the body. Continue sewing. Knot off.

A. Insert ribbon tail.

B. Attach elephant top.

7. Using 1 strand of gray floss, blanket stitch the patterned big ear pieces to the felt big ear pieces. *C*

8. Whipstitch the ears to the elephant body. Knot off at the base of an ear. *D*

9. Using the baby elephant pattern pieces, repeat Steps 1–8 to complete Baby Elephant.

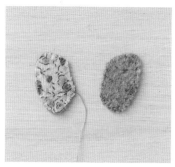

C. Stitch felt and fabric ear pieces together.

D. Attach the elephant ears.

ELEPHANT LOVE *Patterns*

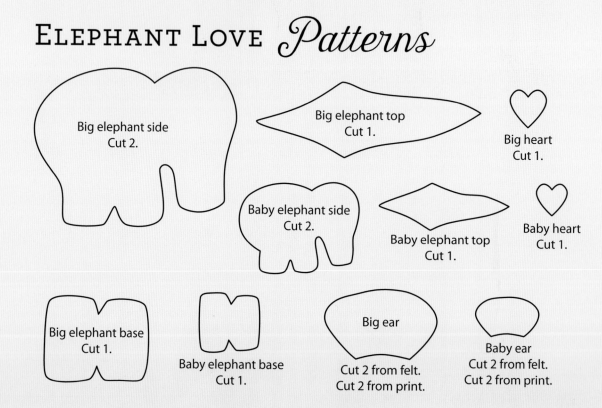

Big elephant side
Cut 2.

Big elephant top
Cut 1.

Big heart
Cut 1.

Baby elephant side
Cut 2.

Baby elephant top
Cut 1.

Baby heart
Cut 1.

Big elephant base
Cut 1.

Baby elephant base
Cut 1.

Big ear
Cut 2 from felt.
Cut 2 from print.

Baby ear
Cut 2 from felt.
Cut 2 from print.

PIPSQUEAKS—Itsy-Bitsy Felt Creations to Stitch & Love

Blushing Bunnies and Kitties

These rosy-cheeked animals are blushing with happiness. Try making them with different colored felt and fabric scraps. They'll look cute no matter what colors or fabrics you decide to use.

Finished sizes:

Mother Bunny: 1⅜″ wide × 2⅜″ high × ¾″ deep (3.5 cm × 6 cm × 2 cm)

Baby Bunny: ¾″ wide × 1⅜″ high × ⅜″ deep (2 cm × 3.5 cm × 1 cm)

Mother Kitty: 1⅜″ wide × 2″ high × ¾″ deep, plus 1⅛″ tail
(3.5 cm × 5 cm × 2 cm, plus 3 cm tail)

Baby Kitty: ¾″ wide × 1⅛″ high × ⅜″ deep, plus ⅝″ tail
(2 cm × 3 cm × 1 cm, plus 1.5 cm tail)

materials

- **Gray felt:** 4¾˝ × 8˝ (12 cm × 20.5 cm)

- **Cream felt:** 4¾˝ × 8˝ (12 cm × 20.5 cm)

- **Pink felt:** 1¾˝ × 1¾˝ (4.5 cm × 4.5 cm)

- **Patterned fabric A:** 2½˝ × 2½˝ (6.5 cm × 6.5 cm)

- **Patterned fabric B:** 1¼˝ × 1¼˝ (3.25 cm × 3.25 cm)

- **Patterned fabric C:** 1¼˝ × 1¼˝ (3.25 cm × 3.25 cm)

- **12 small black round beads:** ⅛˝ (0.3 cm)

- **Embroidery floss:** gray, white, black, pink, and colors to match fabrics

- **Polyfill**

- **3 mini pompoms**

cutting

Refer to the project patterns (page 52) and Tracing and Cutting Pattern Pieces (page 10). Refer to Using a Tear-Away Template for Embroidery (page 11) for the embroidery details.

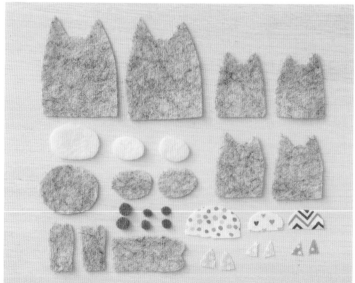

Bunny and kitty felt pieces

From the gray felt, cut:

- 2 big kitty bodies
- 4 small kitty bodies
- 1 big kitty tail
- 2 small kitty tails
- 1 big base
- 2 small bases
- 1 big face
- 2 small faces

From the cream felt, cut:

- 2 big bunny bodies
- 4 small bunny bodies
- 1 big base
- 2 small bases
- 1 big face
- 2 small faces

From the pink felt, cut free-form (or hole-punch)

- 12 small circles for cheeks

From patterned fabric A, cut:

- 2 big tummies
- 2 big bunny ears
- 2 big kitty ears

From patterned fabric B, cut:

- 2 small tummies
- 2 small bunny ears
- 2 small kitty ears

From patterned fabric C, cut:

- 2 small tummies
- 2 small bunny ears
- 2 small kitty ears

CONSTRUCTION

Refer to Construction Basics (page 6) and Glossary of Stitches (page 15). Unless stated otherwise, use 1 strand of matching floss for appliqué stitches and 2 strands of matching floss for blanket stitches.

Bunnies

1. Using 1 strand of matching floss, appliqué the big ears, big tummy, and big face onto a big bunny body.

Appliqué bunny ears, tummy, and face.

2. Using 1 strand of black floss, sew beads in place for eyes and embroider whiskers, mouth, and nose line. Make a tiny cross-stitch for the belly button. *A*

3. Appliqué cheeks onto the face and satin stitch a small triangular nose. *B*

4. Blanket stitch the big bunny bodies together, starting from a lower corner. Stop when you get to the opposite lower corner (But don't knot off just yet!). *C*

5. Blanket stitch the big base piece to the big bunny body. Leave a gap, stuff with polyfill, and continue sewing. Knot off. *D*

6. For a tail, sew a mini pompom onto the back of the bunny. *E*

7. Using the small bunny pattern pieces, follow Steps 1–6 to complete each Baby Bunny.

A. Attach eyes and embroider facial details.

B. Sew cheeks and nose.

C. Blanket stitch body pieces together.

D. Attach base; stuff.

E. Attach a pompom tail.

Kitties

1. To make the big kitty tail, fold it in half and blanket stitch the sides together, using 1 strand of matching floss. Knot off. Set aside. *A*

2. Using the big kitty pieces, follow construction Steps 1–4 for Bunnies (pages 49 and 50). *B*

3. Insert the big kitty tail at the center back. Blanket stitch the big base piece to the kitty body, making sure you securely whipstitch the tail in place as you sew. Before finishing, stuff with polyfill. Finish stitching and knot off. *C*

4. Using the small kitty pattern pieces, repeat Steps 1–3 to complete each Baby Kitty.

A. Fold and sew kitty tail.

B. Kitty body detail

C. Insert kitty tail

BLUSHING BUNNIES AND KITTIES *Patterns*

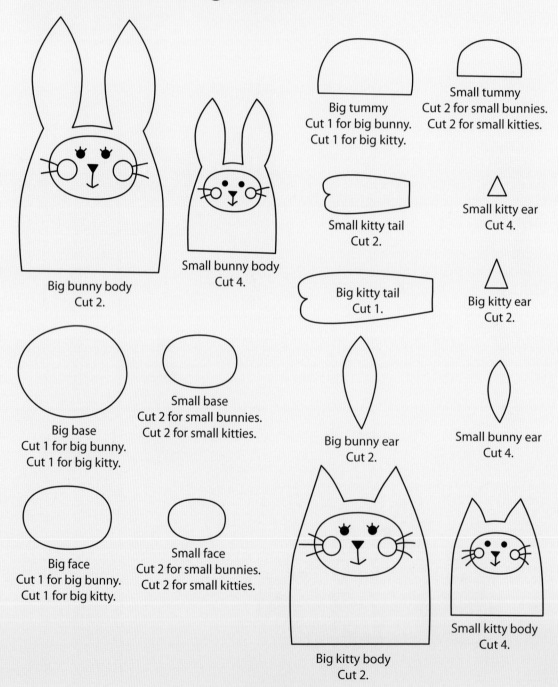

Big bunny body
Cut 2.

Small bunny body
Cut 4.

Big tummy
Cut 1 for big bunny.
Cut 1 for big kitty.

Small tummy
Cut 2 for small bunnies.
Cut 2 for small kitties.

Small kitty tail
Cut 2.

Small kitty ear
Cut 4.

Big kitty tail
Cut 1.

Big kitty ear
Cut 2.

Big base
Cut 1 for big bunny.
Cut 1 for big kitty.

Small base
Cut 2 for small bunnies.
Cut 2 for small kitties.

Big bunny ear
Cut 2.

Small bunny ear
Cut 4.

Big face
Cut 1 for big bunny.
Cut 1 for big kitty.

Small face
Cut 2 for small bunnies.
Cut 2 for small kitties.

Big kitty body
Cut 2.

Small kitty body
Cut 4.

Koala in a Gum-Leaf Bed

This little koala is rather shy and likes to hide inside his gum-leaf bed. Can you coax him out to play?

Finished sizes:

Koala: 1⅛″ wide × 1⅝″ high × ⅜″ deep (3 cm × 4 cm × 1 cm)

Gum-Leaf Bed: 2″ wide × 5⅛″ high × ⅜″ deep (5 cm × 13 cm × 1 cm)

materials

- **Leaf green felt:** 6″ × 8¾″ (15.25 cm × 22.25 cm)

- **Gray felt:** 2″ × 3½″ (5 cm × 9 cm)

- **White felt:** 2″ × 2″ (5 cm × 5 cm)

- **Bright pink felt:** 1″ × 2¼″ (2.5 cm × 5.75 cm)

- **Chocolate brown felt:** 2″ × 2″ (5 cm × 5 cm)

- **2 small black round beads:** ⅛″ (0.3 cm)

- **7 yellow seed beads**

- **Embroidery floss:** leaf green, gray, white, bright pink, chocolate brown, and black

- **Polyfill**

cutting

Refer to the project patterns (page 57) and Tracing and Cutting Pattern Pieces (page 10).

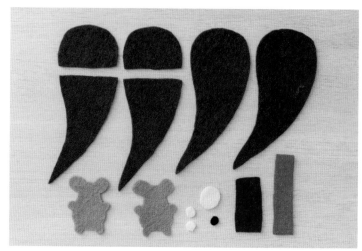

Koala and gum leaf felt pieces

From the leaf green felt, cut:

- 2 leaf backs

- 2 leaf tops

- 2 leaf tips

From the gray felt, cut:

- 2 bodies

From the white felt, cut:

- 2 ears

- 1 tummy

From the bright pink felt, cut:

- 1 blossom

From the chocolate brown felt, cut:

- 1 nose (free-form or pattern)

- 1 leaf stem

CONSTRUCTION

Refer to Construction Basics (page 6) and Glossary of Stitches (page 15). Unless stated otherwise, use 1 strand of matching floss for appliqué and running stitches and 2 strands of matching floss for blanket stitches.

Gum Leaf

Finished gum leaf

1. Fold the leaf stem in half and blanket stitch long sides together. Knot off.

Stitch leaf stem.

2. Pair together the leaf backs, leaf tops, and leaf tips. Using 2 strands of chocolate brown floss, backstitch a line down the center of each.

Backstitch lines through leaf pieces.

3. Aligning the outer edges, place the leaf tip and leaf top on top of the leaf back. Insert the stem at the top. Blanket stitch around the outside edges, including the flat edges of the leaf tips and tops. Make sure you securely whipstitch the stem in place as you sew. Knot off.

4. Fold the blossom piece in half. Using 2 strands of matching floss, stitch the long edges together with a gathering stitch. Pull the thread gently so it gathers the felt into a ring shape. Stitch the ends together. Knot off.

5. Using embroidery scissors, make short even snips around the outer edge of the blossom. Position the blossom on the leaf and stitch in place. Sew a few yellow beads into the center of the blossom. Knot off.

Fold and stitch blossom.

Gather blossom.

Stitch blossom into place with beads.

Koala

Finished koala

A. Appliqué tummy, ears, and nose.

1. Appliqué the tummy, ears, and nose onto a koala body piece. *A*

2. Using 1 strand of black floss, sew black beads in place for eyes and embroider a tiny cross-stitch mouth and bellybutton. *B*

3. Using 1 strand of matching floss, blanket stitch the 2 koala body pieces together. Before finishing, stuff with a small amount of polyfill. Finish stitching and knot off.

B. Close-up of koala eyes and mouth

Koala in a Gum-Leaf Bed
Patterns

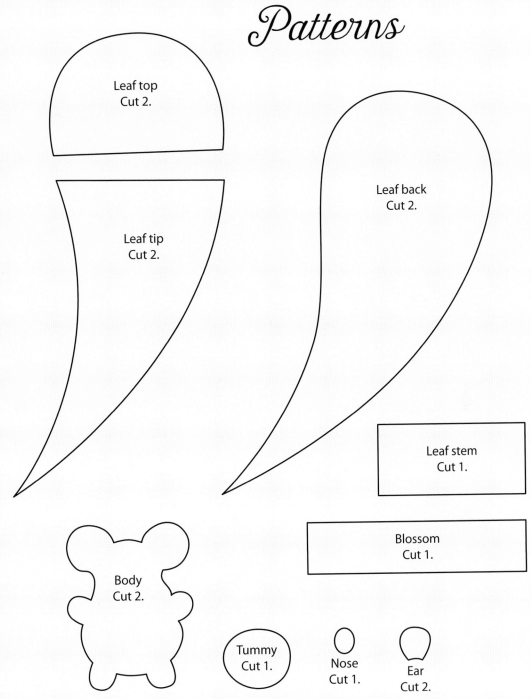

Leaf top
Cut 2.

Leaf back
Cut 2.

Leaf tip
Cut 2.

Leaf stem
Cut 1.

Blossom
Cut 1.

Body
Cut 2.

Tummy
Cut 1.

Nose
Cut 1.

Ear
Cut 2.

Chirpy Chickens

Pa and Ma Chicken are proud parents of three chirpy cheeky chicks.

Finished sizes:

Pa Chicken: 2½″ wide × 2⅜″ high × ¾″ deep (6.5 cm × 6 cm × 2 cm)

Ma Chicken: 2⅜″ wide × 2″ high × ¾″ deep (6 cm × 5 cm × 2 cm)

Chick: 1⅜″ wide × ¾″ high × ⅜″ deep (3.5 cm × 2 cm × 1 cm)

58

materials

- **Cream felt:** 3¼˝ × 4˝ (8.25 cm × 10 cm)

- **Brown felt:** 3¼˝ × 4˝ (8.25 cm × 10 cm)

- **Beige felt:** 2¾˝ × 2¾˝ (7 cm × 7 cm)

- **Yellow felt:** 3¼˝ × 4˝ (8.25 cm × 10 cm)

- **Red felt:** 1¼˝ × 2½˝ (3.25 cm × 6.5 cm)

- **Orange felt:** 1¼˝ × 1¼˝ (3.25 cm × 3.25 cm)

- **10 small black round beads:** ⅛˝ (0.3 cm)

- **Embroidery floss:** cream, brown, beige, yellow, orange, and black

- **Polyfill**

cutting

Refer to the project patterns (page 62) and Tracing and Cutting Pattern Pieces (page 10).

Chicken felt pieces

From the cream felt, cut:

- 2 Pa bodies

- 1 Pa base

- 1 Ma face

From the brown felt, cut:

- 2 Ma bodies

- 1 Ma base

- 2 Pa wings

From the beige felt, cut:

- 2 Ma wings

- 1 Pa face

From the yellow felt, cut:

- 6 chick bodies

- 6 chick wings

- 3 chick bases

From the red felt, cut:

- 1 Pa comb

- 1 Ma comb

- 1 Pa throat

- 1 Ma throat

From the orange felt, cut:

- 2 big beaks

- 3 small beaks

CONSTRUCTION

Refer to Construction Basics (page 6) and Glossary of Stitches (page 15). Unless stated otherwise, use 1 strand of matching floss for appliqué and running stitches and 2 strands of matching floss for blanket stitches.

Pa Chicken

1. Appliqué a Pa Chicken face to a Pa Chicken body piece. Tuck the Pa Chicken throat piece under as you sew. *A*

2. Using 2 strands of black floss, sew beads in place for eyes. Using 1 strand of orange floss, backstitch across the center of a big beak piece. *B*

A. Appliqué Pa Chicken's face.

B. Pa Chicken facial details

3. Insert the Pa wings and the Pa comb in place between the Pa Chicken body pieces. Blanket stitch the body pieces together, making sure you securely whipstitch the wing and comb in place as you sew. *C*

4. Blanket stitch the Pa Chicken base to the body. Before finishing, stuff with polyfill. Finish stitching and knot off. *D*

C. Sew body, wings, and comb together.

D. Sew chicken base to body and stuff.

Ma Chicken

Using the Ma Chicken pattern pieces, follow the Pa Chicken construction Steps 1–4 (page 60).

Ma Chicken construction

Chicks

1. Using 2 strands of black floss, sew black beads in place for eyes on 3 of the chick bodies. Appliqué the small beak piece into place. *A*

2. Using 1 strand of matching floss, blanket stitch the chick body pieces together. As you stitch, insert the chick wings and securely whipstitch them in place. *B*

3. Blanket stitch a chick base to the body. Before finishing, stuff with polyfill. Finish stitching and knot off.

4. Repeat Steps 1–3 to make the remaining 2 chicks.

A. Chick facial details

B. Stitch chick body pieces together.

CHIRPY CHICKENS
Patterns

Pa body
Cut 2.

Pa wing
Cut 2.

Pa comb
Cut 1.

Pa throat
Cut 1.

Pa base
Cut 1.

Pa face
Cut 1.

Big beak
Cut 2.

Ma body
Cut 2.

Ma wing
Cut 2.

Ma comb
Cut 1.

Ma throat
Cut 1.

Ma base
Cut 1.

Ma face
Cut 1.

Chick body
Cut 6.

Chick wing
Cut 6.

Chick base
Cut 3.

Small beak
Cut 3.

PIPSQUEAKS—Itsy-Bitsy Felt Creations to Stitch & Love

Mister Mousy

Mister Mousy is a pint-sized rodent. He looks smart in his red jacket, but looks adorable in other colors too. Mister Mousy also likes to hold tiny objects, such as cupcakes, ice-cream cones, or strawberries.

Finished size: 1⅛˝ wide × 1⅝˝ high × 1˝ deep, plus 3⅛˝ tail
(3 cm × 4 cm × 2.5 cm, plus 8 cm tail)

materials

- **Gray felt:** 4″ × 4¾″ (10 cm × 12 cm)

- **White felt:** 1¾″ × 1¾″ (4.5 cm × 4.5 cm)

- **Red felt:** 2¾″ × 2¾″ (7 cm × 7 cm)

- **2 small black round beads:** ⅛″ (0.3 cm)

- **1 pink seed bead**

- **Embroidery floss:** gray, white, black, red, and pale pink

- **Polyfill**

- **Rice**

- **Fishing line or beading thread:** 8″ (20 cm)

cutting

Refer to the project patterns (page 70) and Tracing and Cutting Pattern Pieces (page 10).

Mousy felt pieces

From the gray felt, cut:

- 1 body

- 1 tail

- 1 head

- 1 base

- 2 paws

- 2 feet

From the white felt, cut:

- 1 front

From the red felt, cut:

- 1 jacket

- 2 sleeves

CONSTRUCTION

Refer to Construction Basics (page 6) and Glossary of Stitches (page 15). Unless stated otherwise, use 1 strand of matching floss for whipstitches and 2 strands of matching floss for blanket stitches.

1. To make the tail, fold it in half and blanket stitch the sides and short ends together, using 1 strand of matching floss. Knot off. Repeat with both paws. Set aside. *A*

2. Fold the head in half symmetrically, and blanket stitch the straight edges together. Turn the head inside out, so the stitches are on the inside. (The pointy part will be the nose.) *B & C*

3. Fold the curved edge of the head toward the opposite edge, aligning the center curved edge with the opposite edge. Starting at the center, blanket stitch toward 1 ear. Do not knot off. Stuff the head with polyfill. Bring the needle back to the center and blanket stitch the edge toward the opposite ear. Make 3–4 backstitches along the side of each ear to make them more prominent. This also helps hide any polyfill that might be visible through the ears. Knot off. *D–F*

A. Fold and stitch tail and paws.

B. Fold and stitch head.

C. Turn head inside out.

D. Stitch toward mousy ears; stuff.

E. Stitched mouse head

F. Stitch around each mouse ear.

4. Using 2 strands of black floss, sew black beads in place for eyes. Bring the needle down to the mouth position and make a single stitch. Bring the needle to the underside of the head and knot off. Using 2 strands of pale pink floss, sew a pink bead in place for the nose. Knot off. Set the mousy head aside. *G*

G. Mouse eyes, mouth, and nose

5. Blanket stitch the mousy front and body together along one edge. Knot off. Repeat on the opposite side. Turn the body inside out. *H & I*

6. Whipstitch the base piece to the body. As you stitch, insert the tail at the center back and the 2 feet at the center front, making sure you securely whipstitch them in place as you sew. To knot off, bring the needle through to the middle of the back. The jacket will eventually hide the knot. *J*

7. Spoon rice through the top opening of the mouse body until about half full. Stuff the remaining space with polyfill until the body is plump.

H. Stitch front and body together.   I. Turn inside out.

J. Sew base, tail, and feet in place.

PIPSQUEAKS—Itsy-Bitsy Felt Creations to Stitch & Love

8. With 2 strands of matching floss, make a gathering stitch around the neck of the body. Pull gently until the edges come together. Do not knot off. **K**

9. Sew the head onto the body by inserting the needle into the bottom of the head and then through the top of the body several times. Moving around the head, stitch until the head is securely attached. Take the needle through to the middle back of the mouse body. Knot off. Set aside. **L**

10. Wrap a sleeve around a mousy paw and fold over. Using 1 strand of matching floss, blanket stitch the bottom edges of the sleeve together. Knot off. Repeat with the second sleeve and paw. **M**

K. Gather and close the neck opening.

L. Stitch head to body.

M. Sew sleeves around paws.

11. Using 1 strand of matching floss, whipstitch the first sleeve/paw unit to the mousy jacket piece. Make sure it protrudes over the side edge of the jacket. Whipstitch the second sleeve/paw unit to the opposite side of the jacket.

Fold the top edge of the jacket over to make a collar. Sew in place with a running stitch. **N**

12. Place the jacket around the mouse body. Using 2 strands of matching floss, sew the jacket in place. Push the needle from 1 side of the jacket (in the armpit area), through the body, to the opposite side of the jacket. Repeat until the jacket is secure. Knot off. **O**

N. Attach sleeves and stitch collar.

O. Attach jacket to the mouse.

13. *Optional:* Sew the paws together, or sew a tiny item such as a cupcake (page 76), strawberry (page 85), ice-cream cone (page 92) or teddy (page 81) into the mouse paws.

14. Thread a needle with fishing line/beading thread. Double over and tie a knot at one end, making sure you have two lovely long whiskers. Insert the needle through the nose area. Carefully tie a knot on the other side. Pull tight and trim the whiskers.

Close-up of mousy whiskers

Mousies ready for fun! Add tiny items from other projects.

MISTER MOUSY *Patterns*

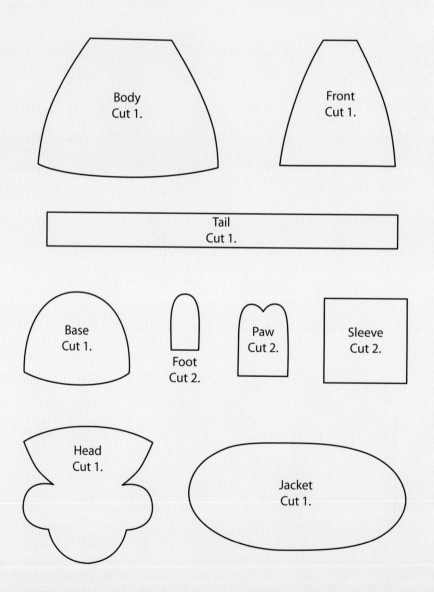

Body
Cut 1.

Front
Cut 1.

Tail
Cut 1.

Base
Cut 1.

Foot
Cut 2.

Paw
Cut 2.

Sleeve
Cut 2.

Head
Cut 1.

Jacket
Cut 1.

PIPSQUEAKS—*Itsy-Bitsy Felt Creations to Stitch & Love*

utterly pipsqueak

⅜″–¾″ (1 cm–2 cm)

A dash of patience, some practice, and a detailed eye are recommended for these teensy projects. Cut and sew carefully—the results are well worth the effort! Many of these tiny items are suitable play companions for any critter featured within this book. Mister Mousy (page 63) might like a dainty pet dog (page 88), or perhaps the Chirpy Chickens (page 58) will enjoy a cupcake picnic (page 76).

Happy Birthday Cakes

Chocolate, banana, vanilla, strawberry, orange ...
what flavor cake will you make? Tiny critters will enjoy these party cakes.

Finished size: 1⅛″ diameter × ⅝″ high (3 cm diameter × 1.5 cm)

materials

- **Cake layer, felt color A:** 3¼″ × 4″ (8.25 cm × 10 cm)

- **Cake filling layer, felt color B:** 1½″ × 3″ (3.75 cm × 7.5 cm)

- **Cake filling layer, felt color C:** 1½″ × 3″ (3.75 cm × 7.5 cm)

- **Cake frosting layer, felt color D:** 1½″ × 1½″ (3.75 cm × 3.75 cm)

- **Seed beads:** red, pink, blue, green, yellow, orange, and silver

- **Embroidery floss:** colors to match felt

cutting

Refer to the project patterns (page 75) and Tracing and Cutting Pattern Pieces (page 10).

Cake felt pieces

From felt color A, cut:
- 6 cake layers

From felt color B, cut:
- 1 or 2 fillings

From felt color C, cut:
- 1 or 2 fillings

From felt color D, cut:
- 1 frosting

CONSTRUCTION

Refer to Construction Basics (page 6) and Glossary of Stitches (page 15). Use 1 strand of matching floss for blanket stitches.

Finished 2-layer cake

Finished 3-layer cake

1. Start with 6 cake layer pieces. For a 2-layer cake, divide the pieces into 2 stacks of 3. For a 3-layer cake, divide into 3 stacks of 2. Blanket stitch around each pair or triple-layer set. Knot off.

Blanket stitch around each set of cake layers.

2. Put the cake frosting on a layer piece. Using 1 strand of matching floss and stitching through both the frosting and layer pieces, attach beads or decorate with embroidery stitches.

Examples of decorated cake frosting

3. Stack the cake layers, filling pieces, and frosted top. Use a plain layer, 1 or 2 fillings, and a decorated top layer for a 2-layer cake. Use 2 plain layers, 2 fillings, and a decorated top layer for a 3-layer cake.

Assemble cake layers, filling, and frosting.

4. Using 2 strands of floss that matches the outer layers, start from the bottom layer and push the needle to the underside of the top layer. Hide the starting knot within the bottom layer. Carefully, push the needle back down to catch the top side of the bottom layer. Repeat this process until you have stitched around the entire cake. Knot off within one of the layers.

tip If you prefer not to sew, then glue the layers together!

Stitch cake layers together. Use matching floss.

HAPPY BIRTHDAY CAKES *Patterns*

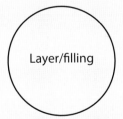

Layer/filling

Frosting
Cut 1.

Cut 6 for cake layer.
Cut 1 or 2 for first filling.
Cut 1 or 2 for second filling.

Time for a Picnic

Have you ever seen such a small picnic?
Tiny critters will enjoy a cupcake feast.

Finished sizes:

Cupcake: ⅜˝ diameter × ⅜˝ high (1 cm diameter × 1 cm)

Plate: 1¼˝ diameter × ⅛˝ high (3.25 cm diameter × 0.3 cm)

Picnic Rug: 3⅞˝ × 3⅞˝ (10 cm × 10 cm)

materials

- **Beige felt:** 3¼″ × 1¾″ (8.25 cm × 4.5 cm)
- **White felt:** 4″ × 4″ (10 cm × 10 cm)
- **Pale pink felt:** ¾″ × ¾″ (2 cm × 2 cm)
- **Bright pink felt:** ¾″ × ¾″ (2 cm × 2 cm)
- **Mint green felt:** ¾″ × ¾″ (2 cm × 2 cm)
- **Chocolate brown felt:** ¾″ × ¾″ (2 cm × 2 cm)
- **Lilac felt:** ¾″ × ¾″ (2 cm × 2 cm)
- **Cotton fabric with woven gingham check:** 4¼″ × 4¼″ (10.75 cm × 10.75 cm)
- **Seed beads:** red, pink, silver, yellow, and green
- **Embroidery floss:** bright blue, beige, white, pale pink, bright pink, mint green, chocolate brown, and lilac
- **Polyfill**

cutting

Refer to the project patterns (page 80) and Tracing and Cutting Pattern Pieces (page 10).

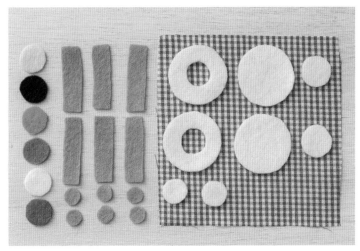

Picnic felt pieces

From the beige felt, cut:

- 6 cupcake sides
- 6 cupcake bottoms

From the white felt, cut:

- 2 whole plates
- 2 plate rings
- 2 inner plates
- 2 plate bottoms
- 1 cupcake top

From each pale pink, bright pink, mint green, chocolate brown, and lilac felt, cut:

- 1 cupcake top

From the woven gingham, cut even with the check:

- 1 square 4″ × 4″ (10 cm × 10 cm)

CONSTRUCTION

Refer to Construction Basics (page 6) and Glossary of Stitches (page 15). Use 1 strand of matching floss for blanket stitches, running stitches, and whipstitches.

Cupcakes

1. Blanket stitch the short sides of a cupcake side together. Turn inside out so the stitched seam is on the inside. *A & B*

2. Blanket stitch the cupcake bottom to the base of the cupcake side. Knot off. Set aside. *C*

3. Using 1 strand of floss, decorate the cupcake tops with seed beads, French knots, or scattered seed stitches. *D*

4. Blanket stitch the cupcake top to the cupcake side, using thread that matches the cupcake top. Before finishing, stuff with polyfill. Finish stitching and knot off. *E*

5. Repeat Steps 1–4 to make 6 cupcakes.

A. Sew short sides together.

B. Turn cupcake side inside out.

C. Sew cupcake bottom to cupcake side.

D. Decorate cupcake tops.

E. Sew cupcake top to side, and stuff.

PIPSQUEAKS—Itsy-Bitsy Felt Creations to Stitch & Love

Plates

1. Using 2 strands of bright blue floss, embroider a design around the plate ring. I used 6 clusters of 3 scattered seed stitches. *A*

2. Whipstitch the small inner plate to the center of the plate ring. *B*

3. Blanket stitch the plate ring to a whole plate piece. *C*

4. Use a running stitch to sew the plate bottom to the whole plate piece. *D*

5. Repeat Steps 1–4 to make a second plate.

Finished plate

A. Embroider plate ring design.

B. Sew small inner plate to center of plate ring.

C. Sew plate ring to whole plate.

D. Attach plate bottom.

Picnic Rug

Using a needle or pin, remove threads from each side until the fabric is fringed.

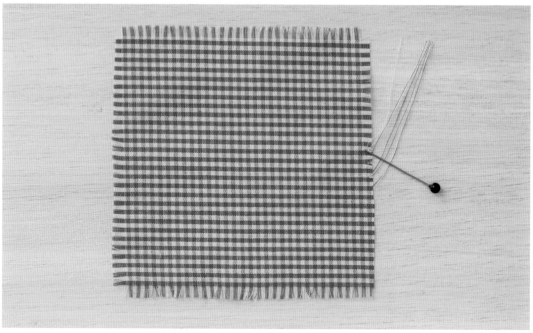

Fringe the fabric.

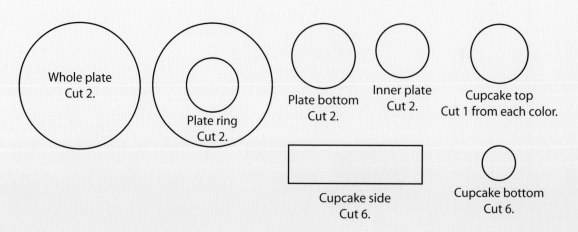

TIME FOR A PICNIC *Patterns*

Whole plate
Cut 2.

Plate ring
Cut 2.

Plate bottom
Cut 2.

Inner plate
Cut 2.

Cupcake top
Cut 1 from each color.

Cupcake side
Cut 6.

Cupcake bottom
Cut 6.

Teeny-Weeny Bear

Teeny-weeny Bear is, well ... teeny weeny. This tiny teddy bear makes a cute toy for a felt critter, but can also be adapted to make a set of earrings or a brooch. Try making Teeny-Weeny in various colors.

Finished size: 1″ wide × 1″ high × ⅜″ deep (2.5 cm × 2.5 cm × 1 cm)

materials

- **Blue felt:** 1¾″ × 2¾″ (4.5 cm × 7 cm)
- **Cream felt:** ¾″ × ¾″ (2 cm × 2 cm)
- **Red felt:** ¾″ × ¾″ (2 cm × 2 cm)
- **Embroidery floss:** blue, cream, and black
- **Polyfill**
- **Earring findings** *(optional)*: ¾″ (2 cm)
- **Brooch pin/safety pin** *(optional)*: ⅜″ (1 cm) or ⅝″ (1.5 cm)

cutting

Refer to the project patterns (page 84) and Tracing and Cutting Pattern Pieces (page 10).

Bear felt pieces

From blue felt, cut:

- 2 bodies

From cream felt, cut:

- 1 face

From red felt, cut:

- 1 bowtie

CONSTRUCTION

Refer to Construction Basics (page 6) and Glossary of Stitches (page 15).
Use 1 strand of matching floss for appliqué and blanket stitches.

1. Appliqué the face to a bear body. *A*

2. Using 1 strand of black floss, embroider 2 French knots for eyes, satin stitch a triangular nose, and make 2 diagonal straight stiches for a mouth. *B*

3. Place a bowtie underneath the bear face. Using 1 strand of black floss, loop a stitch around the middle of the bowtie. Pull tight. Make a few more stitches around the bowtie, attaching the bowtie to the bear. Knot off. *C*

4. Blanket stitch the body pieces together. Before finishing, stuff with a tiny amount of polyfill. Finish stitching and knot off behind the bowtie. *D*

A. Sew face to body.

B. Embroider facial features.

C. Attach bowtie to bear.

D. Blanket stitch around bear; stuff.

TEENY-WEENY BEAR
Patterns

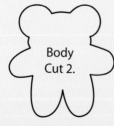

Body
Cut 2.

Face
Cut 1.

Bowtie
Cut 1.

PIPSQUEAKS—Itsy-Bitsy Felt Creations to Stitch & Love

Strawberry Earrings

This strawberry earring set is a sweet decorative accessory. Tiny felt critters also enjoy picking these strawberries for pint-sized picnics.

Finished size: ⅜˝ diameter × ⅜˝ high (1 cm diameter × 1 cm)

materials

- **Red felt:** 1¾˝ × 2˝ (4.5 cm × 5 cm)
- **Green felt:** 1˝ × 1¾˝ (2.5 cm × 4.5 cm)
- **Embroidery floss:** red, white, and green
- **Polyfill**
- **2 French-hook earring findings:** ¾˝ (2 cm)

cutting

Refer to the project patterns (page 87) and Tracing and Cutting Pattern Pieces (page 10).

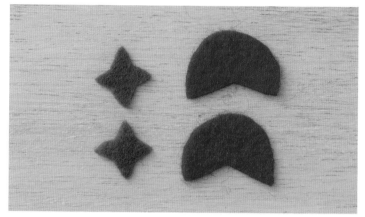

Strawberry felt pieces

From the red felt, cut:

- 2 strawberries

From the green felt, cut:

- 2 leaves

CONSTRUCTION

Refer to Construction Basics (page 6) and Glossary of Stitches (page 15). Use 1 strand of matching floss for running stitches and blanket stitches.

1. Using 2 strands of white floss, sew scattered seed stitches over the strawberry pieces. Knot off.

Sew scattered seed stitches onto strawberries.

2. Fold one strawberry piece in half. Blanket stitch the sides together along the edge. Make a secure knot at the top, but don't cut the thread. *A*

3. Make gathering stitches around the top edge of the strawberry. Carefully pull the thread so the strawberry gathers. Stuff a tiny amount of polyfill inside the strawberry. Knot off. *B & C*

4. Attach a leaf by making a whipstitch at each inside point of the leaf. Firmly stitch an earring finding in place. Knot off. *D & E*

5. Repeat Steps 2–4 to make the second strawberry earring.

A. Fold and stitch strawberry edge.   **B.** Stitch around strawberry top.

C. Gather and stuff the strawberry.   **D.** Stitch leaf onto strawberry.

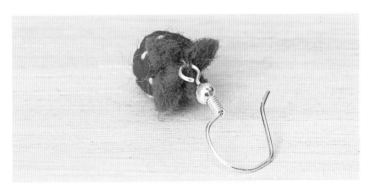

E. Stitch earring finding onto strawberry.

STRAWBERRY EARRINGS *Patterns*

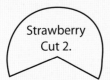

Strawberry
Cut 2.

Leaf
Cut 2.

Dainty Dog

This miniature dog can make a friendly pet for a larger felt critter. It can also be turned into earrings. Try making dogs in different colors and with different patterns.

Finished size (measured from front view): ⅝″ wide × 1″ high × 1⅛″ deep (1.5 cm × 2.5 cm × 3 cm)

materials

- **White felt:** 2½″ × 2½″ (6.5 cm × 6.5 cm)

- **Seed beads:** black and silver

- **Embroidery floss:** white, black, and red

- **Polyfill**

- **Black fabric paint**

cutting

Refer to the project patterns (page 91) and Tracing and Cutting Pattern Pieces (page 10).

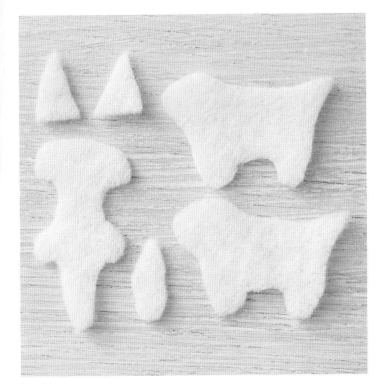

Dog felt pieces

From the white felt, cut:

- 2 bodies

- 1 tummy

- 1 head

- 2 ears (free-form or pattern)

CONSTRUCTION

Refer to Construction Basics (page 6) and Glossary of Stitches (page 15). Use
1 strand of matching floss for appliqué and blanket stitches.

1. Blanket stitch the long half of the tummy
to a body. *A*

tip | *I start sewing from the
dog's back legs.*

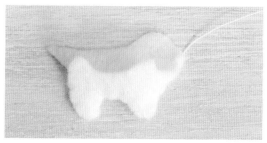

A. Sew tummy to body.

2. Blanket stitch the second body piece to the other half of the tummy. Continue to stitch
all edges together, attaching the dog head at the top with the pointy end toward the nose.
Before finishing, stuff with a small amount of polyfill. Finish stitching and knot off. *B & C*

B. Sew dog body pieces together.

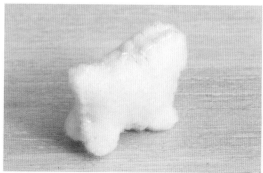

C. Sew dog head piece in place; stuff.

3. Sew the ears in place by taking a single gathering stitch through the base of each ear; then take several overlapping single stitches to attach the ears to the head. *D*

4. Using 1 strand of black floss, sew beads in place for eyes and satin stitch a tiny nose and mouth. *E*

D. Attach dog ears.

E. Attach black eye seed beads, and embroider nose and mouth.

tip | *The best place to knot off is under the neck where the collar will go.*

5. Using 2 strands of red floss, make a stitch through the dog neck. Wind the thread several times around the neck to make the collar. Thread a silver bead in the throat area of the collar. Knot off. *F*

6. *Optional:* Refer to Use Paint for Some Embellishments (page 14) to paint black spots or patches onto the dog body. Allow to dry.

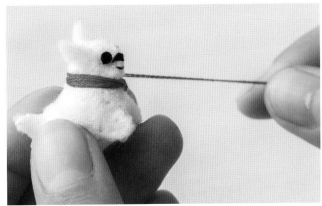

F. Stitch and wrap thread to make collar.

DAINTY DOG *Patterns*

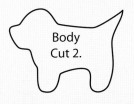
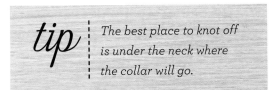
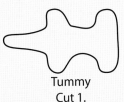

Body
Cut 2.

Ear
Cut 2.

Head
Cut 1.

Tummy
Cut 1.

Ice-Cream Treats

Chocolate, strawberry, vanilla ... what's your favorite ice-cream flavor treat? These tiny ice-creams are a favorite food of felt critters. They also can be turned into earrings.

Finished size: ⅜″ diameter × ¾″ high (1 cm diameter × 2 cm)

materials

- **Beige felt:** 2½″ × 3¼″ (6.5 cm × 8.25 cm)

- **Pale pink felt:** 1½″ × 1½″ (3.75 cm × 3.75 cm)

- **Mint green felt:** 1½″ × 1½″ (3.75 cm × 3.75 cm)

- **White felt:** 1½″ × 1½″ (3.75 cm × 3.75 cm)

- **Lemon yellow felt:** 1½″ × 1½″ (3.75 cm × 3.75 cm)

- **Chocolate brown felt:** 1½″ × 1½″ (3.75 cm × 3.75 cm)

- **Orange felt:** 1½″ × 1½″ (3.75 cm × 3.75 cm)

- **Seed beads:** red, pink, silver, yellow, and green

- **Embroidery floss:** beige, white, pale pink, mint green, chocolate brown, lemon yellow, and orange

- **Polyfill**

- **Earring findings** (*optional*): ¾″ (2 cm)

cutting

Refer to the project patterns (page 94) and Tracing and Cutting Pattern Pieces (page 10).

Ice-cream felt pieces

From the beige felt, cut:

- 6 cones

From each pale pink, mint green, white, lemon yellow, chocolate brown, and orange felt, cut:

- 1 scoop

CONSTRUCTION

Refer to Construction Basics (page 6) and Glossary of Stitches (page 15). Use 1 strand of matching floss for appliqué and blanket stitches.

1. Using 1 strand of matching floss, backstitch a waffle design over an ice-cream cone piece. Knot off. *A*

2. Fold the ice-cream cone in half and blanket stitch the side edges together. Knot off. Stuff with polyfill. *B*

3. Decorate the ice-cream scoops with seed beads, French knots, or scattered seed stitches (or leave plain). *C*

4. Using a strand of matching floss, make a gathering stitch around the outer edge of an ice-cream scoop. Pull gently, stuff with polyfill, and gather the felt to make a round ice-cream scoop. Knot off. *D & E*

5. Whipstitch the scoop to the cone, using 1 strand of beige floss (to match the cone). Knot off. *F*

6. Repeat Steps 1–4 to make 6 ice-cream cones.

A. Backstitch a waffle cone design.

B. Fold and stitch the ice-cream cone edge.

C. Decorate ice-cream scoops.

D. Stitch around scoop edge.

E. Gather to make a scoop.

F. Attach ice-cream scoop to cone.

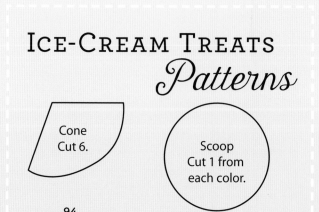

ICE-CREAM TREATS
Patterns

Cone
Cut 6.

Scoop
Cut 1 from each color.

PIPSQUEAKS—Itsy-Bitsy Felt Creations to Stitch & Love

ABOUT THE AUTHOR

Sally Dixon is an Australian girl who loves to create. She owns and runs a small business called Razzle Dazzle Creations. Her imaginative, tiny, and playful designs can be found in her online shops.

Gum trees line the road outside her home in Adelaide, South Australia; the occasional koala stops to snooze in these trees.

Photo by Bec Barnes

She's a trained early childhood teacher, but has worn many hats. She once worked as a pastry chef and loves baking cakes…but must stop eating them! In addition to making her tiny playthings, she works as a creative writer. Her stories have been published in various publications, including the Chicken Soup for the Soul books.

Sally Dixon

What else is there to know about Sally? She loves animals (especially cats), there are far too many books in her possession, journeys excite her, Josh Groban's voice melts her heart, and her taste in pop culture ranges from Mr. Darcy to *Star Trek* (with much in between).

sallydixon.com.au

madeit.com.au/razzledazzle

etsy.com/shop/RazzleDazzlebySally

facebook.com/RazzleDazzlebySally

RESOURCES

The first place to go for information and products is your local quilt shop. If that is not possible or they cannot help you, then try the Internet for information.

USA

Ribbons and Twine

Creative Impressions Warehouse
creativeimpressions.com

Cotton Fabric

Timeless Treasures: ttfabrics.com

Scissors, Notions, and Threads

Kreinik Mfg. Co., Inc.: kreinik.com

Jewelry Findings and Other Craft Supplies

Jane Crafts: janecrafts.com

Transfer Iron-on Pens

Sulky of America: sulky.com

Australia

Wool Felt

Winterwood Steiner Inspired Toys
winterwoodtoys.com.au

General Craft Supplies

FOR BROOCH BACKS AND MORE:
D and L Craftworkz: craftworkz.com.au

FOR IRON-ON TRANSFER PENS AND MORE:
Punch with Judy: punchwithjudy.com.au

FOR JEWELRY FINDINGS AND MORE:
Riot Art & Craft: riotstores.com.au

General Craft Supplies

Spotlight: spotlight.com.au

Lincraft: lincraft.com.au

ctpub.com